S0-ABC-061

Zany Riddles

kids
made you laugh!™

Editorial Director: Erin Conley

Designer: Jeanette Miller, Michelle Hill

Special thanks to Suzanne Cracraft, Maria Llull, Kirsty Melville,
Bob Moog, Hillary Osness and Nancy Spector
for their invaluable assistance!

ISBN 1-57528-930-X

10 9 8 7 6 5 4 3 2 1 - 09 08 07 06 05

TABLE OF CONTENTS

ZANY RIDDLES

A Riddle Could Save Your Life
(a maybe-not-so-true-story)

Once upon a time two friends walked into a spooky forest at night.

> *Why did they, you ask?*
> *Because that's what kids do in once-upon-a-timers, silly.*

Well, they got lost and were freaked out. They came to a rushing river, and of course there was a bridge across it, and of course on the other side the sun was shining and there was a sign that pointed toward home. All the two friends needed to do was cross the bridge and they would be safe and happy ever after. But any bridge worth its weight has a terrible troll living under it, hungry for children. And yes, this one had a particularly nasty fellow below it.

Now, as you may or may not know, you can avoid this terrible fate. Trolls are famous riddle lovers. They can't resist a good riddle. If you tell a troll a riddle so goofy, so outrageous, that he groans long enough for you to run across the bridge, then you live to riddle another day. And that's what these kids did. (By the way, that very same riddle is in this book. Which one do you think it is?)

So, know your riddles. And know at least one that will make any old ugly troll groan.

—Erin Anthony

ANIMAL ANTICS

ZANY RIDDLES

ANIMAL ANTICS

1) What kind of biscuits should you give to a dog with fleas?

2) What do you call an asthmatic ferret?

3) Why did the chicken take a bath?

6

Answers: 1. Biscuits made from scratch. 2. Wheezel 3. It smelled fowl.

ANiMAL ANTiCS

4) What can you do to both a chicken and a guitar?

5) Why did the poor mother duck cry after counting her ducklings?

6) What did the parrot say when she wanted a duck for a friend?

ZANY RiDDLES

ANiMAL ANTiCS

⑦ Why won't the male deer cross the street?

⑨ The wolf was wearing sheepskin to blend in with the flock. So why didn't he hunt?

⑧ What did the farmer sing to the sleepy lost lamb?

Answers: 7. The buck stops here.
8. Go to sheep. 9. He was feeling sheepish.

ANIMAL ANTICS

(10) What did one cat say to the cat that missed the mouse?

(11) What did the dog trainer shout when the dogs tried to run away?

(12) When is a dog like a mosquito?

ZANY RIDDLES

Answers: 10. No one's purrfect. 11. Release the hounds! 12. When it's a bloodhound.

(13) What did the dog say after the kid pulled his textbook from its teeth?

(14) Why did the big cat get kicked out of the poker game?

(15) What kind of animal could be a butler?

10

Answers: 13. Hey, you took the words right out of my mouth. 14. He was a cheater. 15. A door mouse

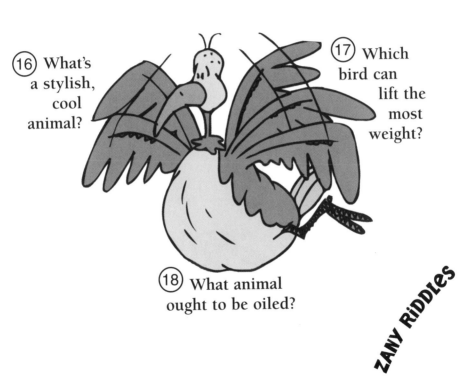

(16) What's a stylish, cool animal?

(17) Which bird can lift the most weight?

(18) What animal ought to be oiled?

ZANY RIDDLES

Answers: 16. A hip-po 17. The crane
18. A mouse—it squeaks.

11

ANIMAL ANTICS

(19) What animal likes to fib?

(20) Which animal doesn't waste its food?

(21) What did the mother goat say to her son when the rabbit was looking at him?

Answers: 19. A lion 20. The giraffe—a little bit goes a long way. 21. Hare's looking at you, kid.

ANIMAL ANTICS

(22) Why was the alley cat sad?

(23) Why did the bird pour oil on himself?

(24) What is both a bird and a part of eating?

ZANY RIDDLES

Answers: 22. Because it was down in the dumps.
23. Because the oily bird catches the worm. 24. Swallow

13

ANiMAL ANTiCS

(25) How do you catch a bird that is one-of-a-kind?

(26) How do you catch a wild bird?

(27) How did the boy owl know the girl owl didn't like him?

Answers: 25. Unique up on it. 26. The tame way. 27. She didn't give a hoot.

ANiMAL ANTiCS

(28) What did the duck say to the farmer feeding him?

(29) How do you catch a squirrel?

(30) What did the mother elephant say when her girl was misbehaving?

ZANY RiDDLES

Answers: 28. Put it on my bill. 29. Climb a tree and act like a nut. 30. Tusk tusk

15

ANIMAL ANTICS

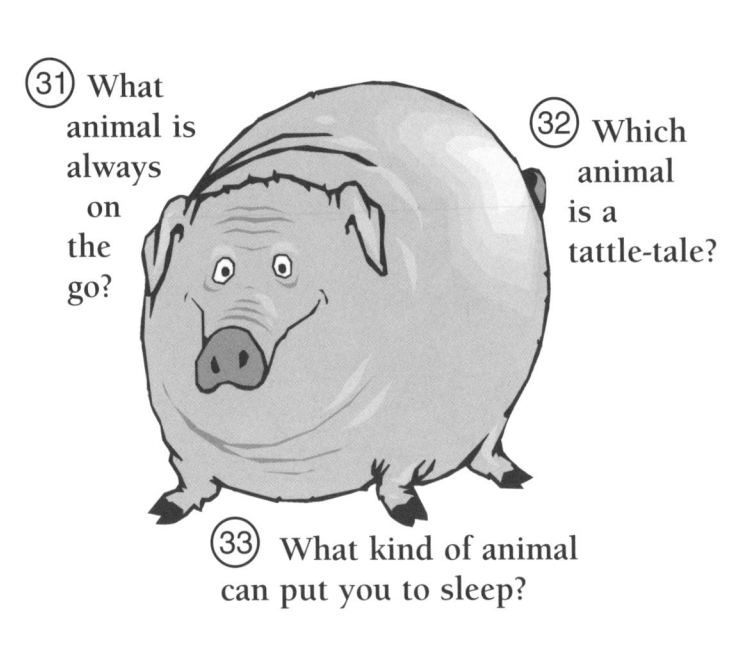

31) What animal is always on the go?

32) Which animal is a tattle-tale?

33) What kind of animal can put you to sleep?

Answers: 31. A go-rilla 32. The pig—it's a squealer. 33. A bore

ANiMAL ANTiCS

(34) What animal can you address fondly?

(35) Which animal has something in common with Homer Simpson?

(36) What did the doe say to the buck about their baby?

ZANY RiDDLES

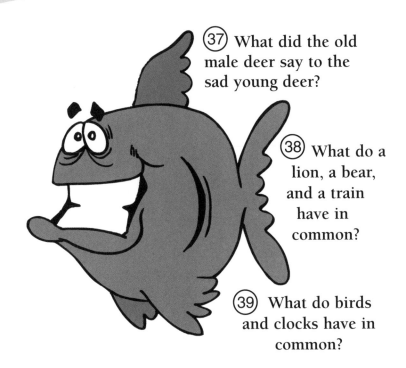

(37) What did the old male deer say to the sad young deer?

(38) What do a lion, a bear, and a train have in common?

(39) What do birds and clocks have in common?

18

Answers: 37. Buck up! 38. They all have tracks. 39. They can be cuckoo.

ANIMAL ANTICS

40 What kind of fish do samurai eat?

41 What fish will make your piano sound good?

42 Why did the chicken jump in the mud puddle, cross the road, and then come back again?

ZANY RIDDLES

Answers: 40. Swordfish 41. Tuna fish 42. She was a dirty double crosser.

43 Why wouldn't the chicken cross the road?

44 Why didn't the turkey cross the road?

45 What do you call a boat full of lambs going to war?

20

46 Why wouldn't the cattle laugh at the jokes?

47 What do you call a polar bear in the desert?

48 Why should fish know what they weigh?

ZANY RIDDLES

Answers: 46. They didn't want to be the laughing stock.
47. Lost 48. They have scales.

21

ANiMAL ANTiCS

(49) What did one reindeer say to the other when he was about to tell a joke?

(50) How many skunks does it take to make a stink?

(51) What did the rattlesnake say to the cobra?

22

ANIMAL ANTICS

52 What does a snake take for a headache?

53 What did the girl boa constrictor say to the boy boa constrictor?

54 What did the buffalo dad say to his boy when he went out to graze?

ANIMAL ANTICS

55) What did the beaver say to the tree?

56) Why couldn't the dog owner believe that her dog brought back the stick?

57) What do you get when you cross a pig and a tree?

Answers: 55. It's been nice gnawing you. 56. Because it was far-fetched. 57. A porcupine

58) What do you get when you cross a shark with a snowman?

59) What do you get when you cross bushes and a pig?

60) What did the sheriff say when he saw rabbits in his jail?

ZANY RIDDLES

Answers: 58. Frostbite 59. A hedgehog 60. We're having a bad hare day.

ANIMAL ANTICS

(61) Why has no one ever spotted a leopard in the wild?

(62) What grows down when it grows up?

(63) When does your shoe look like a very hot dog?

Answers: 61. The leopard already has spots. 62. A goose 63. When its tongue is hanging out.

ANiMAL ANTiCS

(64) What did one skunk say to the other skunk when the hunter came toward them?

(65) Why do sharks swim in salt water?

(66) A parrot that flies away takes what shape?

ZANY RiDDLES

Answers: 64. Let us spray. 65. If they swam in pepper water, they'd sneeze. 66. A polygon

27

ANiMAL ANTiCS

67 What did the hungry fish say to the fisherman?

68 What do you get when you cross a bee and a vulture?

69 Why wouldn't the cowboy ride his girl horse when the sun was out?

28

FOOD FOR THOUGHT

ZANY RIDDLES

FOOD FOR THOUGHT

2 What did one grape say to the other grape at the bottom of the jar?

1 What did the cucumber say when it saw the small pepper in the fridge?

3 Why couldn't the basket of corn learn anything?

Answers: 1. It's a little chili in here. 2. Well, we're in a jam now. 3. Because all the lessons went in one ear and out the other.

(4) What did the boy ear of corn say when he found out the girl ear of corn had a crush on him?

(5) What is the grumpiest fruit?

(6) Why did the salad look sad on Friday night?

ZANY RIDDLES

Answers: 4. Aw, shucks. 5. A crab apple 6. Because it was all dressed up and had nowhere to go.

FOOD FOR THOUGHT

7) Why were the diners disappointed with the nuts?

8) What's a dessert for dads?

9) What kind of tables did the mother want her kid to eat?

Answers: 7. Because they weren't what they were cracked up to be. 8. A Popsicle® 9. Vegetables

FOOD FOR THOUGHT

(10) What kind of nut has no shell?

(11) What's both a dessert and a shoemaker?

(12) What is the nicest fruit?

ZANY RiDDLES

Answers: 10. A doughnut 11. A cobbler 12. A granny apple

FOOD FOR THOUGHT

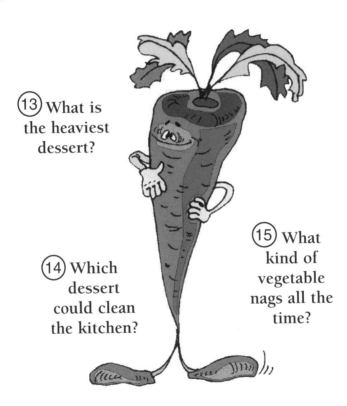

13) What is the heaviest dessert?

14) Which dessert could clean the kitchen?

15) What kind of vegetable nags all the time?

Answers: 13. A marble cake 14. A sponge cake 15. Let us!

FOOD FOR THOUGHT

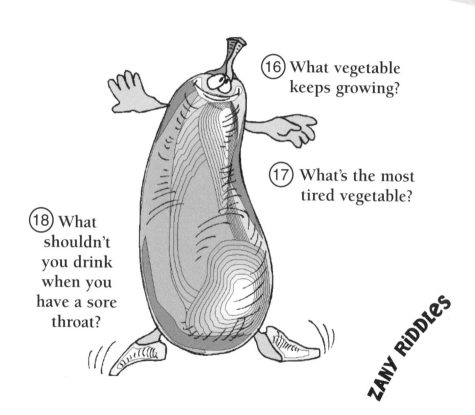

(16) What vegetable keeps growing?

(17) What's the most tired vegetable?

(18) What shouldn't you drink when you have a sore throat?

ZANY RIDDLES

FOOD FOR THOUGHT

19 Why wouldn't the sugar hang out with the honey?

20 When is chicken soup not good for you?

21 What kind of pasta was made today?

Answers: 19. It thought it was too refined. 20. When you're a chicken. 21. New-dles

FOOD FOR THOUGHT

(22) How do you make an eggroll?

(23) What are two things you cannot eat for breakfast?

(24) What had the farmer fed the trembling horse?

Answers: 22. You push it. 23. Lunch and dinner 24. Quaker Oats®

FOOD FOR THOUGHT

25) Why did the baker bake all day and all night?

26) Why did the tiny baker keep telling jokes when he stood on the bread?

27) Why did the silly baker put paper wings into a stick of butter?

Answers: 25. He kneaded the dough. 26. He was on a roll. 27. He was trying to make a butterfly.

FOOD FOR THOUGHT

(28) Why did the hungry Roman wrestler smile when he ate the lioness?

(30) What did the Teddy bear say when the child tried to feed it?

(29) What did the chewing gum say to the shoe?

ZANY RiDDLes

FOOD FOR THOuGHT

(31) What did one candle say to the other candle on the birthday cake?

(33) What did the refrigerator think when it was unplugged?

(32) What's worse than a maggot in the apple you're eating?

Answers: 31. Doesn't this just burn you up? 32. Half a maggot in the apple you're eating. 33. I am going to lose my cool.

GOOFY GHOULS

ZANY RiDDLeS

GOOFY GHOULS

1 How did the sandwich disappear from the beach?

2 What did the lady zombie say about the ugly dress?

3 What did one ghost say to the other ghost who held a rabbit over its head?

Answers: 1. She flew off on her broomstick. 2. I wouldn't be caught dead in that. 3. Now that is hare-raising.

GOOFY GHOULS

④ What does a baby ghost drink?

⑤ Why doesn't Dracula have many friends?

⑥ Why is it easy to fool Dracula?

ZANY RIDDLES

Answers: 4. Evaporated milk 5. He's a pain in the neck.
6. Because he's such a sucker.

43

GOOFY GHOULS

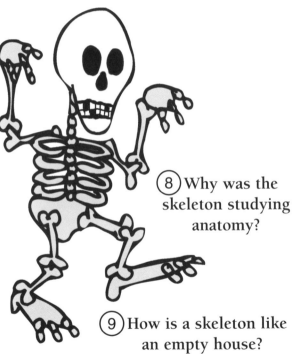

(7) Why couldn't the mummy see the skeleton in the cave?

(8) Why was the skeleton studying anatomy?

(9) How is a skeleton like an empty house?

Answers: 7. There was no body there. 8. He wanted to bone up on the subject. 9. No body's home.

GOOFY GHOULS

(10) What did the girl mummy say to the boy mummy?

(11) Why did the ghost put the night on a diet?

(12) Why was the ghost trying to stay away from the cookies?

ZANY RIDDLES

Answers: 10. I could get wrapped up in you. 11. He wanted to vanish into thin air. 12. He would go right through them.

(13) What did the ghost father say when his son scared the neighbor?

(14) What did one ghoul say to another at the race?

(15) What did the ghoul say to the lifting fog?

Answers: 13. Don't spook unless you're spoken to. 14. You don't stand a ghost of a chance. 15. You'll be missed.

(16) Why were the vampires nervous at the monster poker game?

(17) What is the vampire's favorite dance?

(18) What's a monster's favorite drink?

ZANY RIDDLES

Answers: 16. They were playing for high stakes.
17. The waltz 18. Ghoul-Aid

GOOFY GHOULS

⑲ Which monster can never understand directions?

⑳ What did the father goblin say to the giggling goblin boy in the cemetery?

㉑ Why was the ghost sad?

Answers: 19. A where-wolf 20. Stop laughing—this is a grave matter. 21. Because his haunting license expired.

GOOFY GHOULS

(22) Which monster has bad table manners?

(23) Why didn't the skeleton finish the race?

(24) Why wasn't the mummy a good friend?

ZANY RIDDLES

Answers: 22. The Goblin 23. His heart wasn't in it.
24. Because he was too wrapped up in himself.

GOOFY GHOULS

25) Why was the girl wizard lost?

26) Name a holiday that's both friendly and scary.

27) What position did the phantom play on the soccer team?

50

FReAKs Of NaTuRe

ZANY RiDDLeS

FREAKS OF NATURE

① What happened to the larva that talked and talked?

② What kind of bank has fish instead of money?

③ What has a big mouth but doesn't speak?

Answers: 1. It became a hoarse-fly. 2. A river bank 3. A river

④ What did the beach say to the wave?

⑤ What did one leaf say to another leaf when it saw the lumberjack coming?

⑥ What did one leaf say to the other leaf when the wind started to blow?

ZANY RIDDLES

Answers: 4. You're all washed up. 5. See you in the fall. 6. That's it. I'm leaving.

(7) What did the tree say to the woodpecker?

(8) What did the oak tree say to the pine and maple trees?

(9) What is the most well-liked tree?

54

Answers: 7. You bore me. 8. You two are so sappy. 9. The poplar tree

FREAKS OF NATURE

10 What do flowers and old-fashioned ladies' pants have in common?

12 What did the corn say to the whispering farmer?

sweet Corn

11 What do flowers and bicycles have in common?

ZANY RIDDLES

Answers: 10. They are both bloomers. 11. They both have petals/pedals. 12. I can't ear you.

(13) What did the corn say after the plow crushed it?

(14) What did the boy potato say to the girl potato?

(15) Why was the plant kicked out of the flower shop?

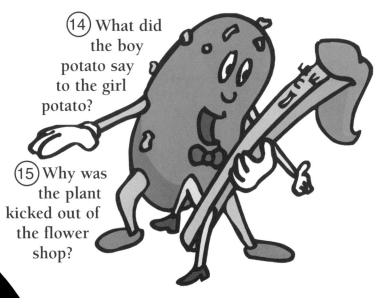

Answers: 13. That took ears off my life. 14. I only have eyes for you. 15. It wasn't making any scents.

16) What happens when a flower has no smell?

17) What did the ivy say to the house?

18) What did the itchy kid yell at the poison ivy?

ZANY RIDDLES

Answers: 16. Non-scents   17. You've got me climbing the walls.   18. That was a rash thing to do!

57

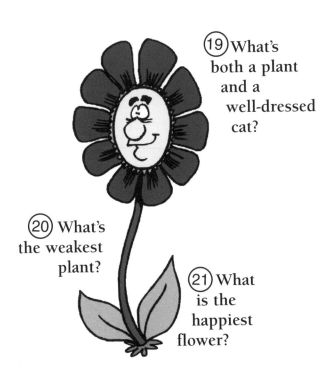

19 What's both a plant and a well-dressed cat?

20 What's the weakest plant?

21 What is the happiest flower?

58

Answers: 19. A dandy-lion 20. A vine, because it can't support itself. 21. The gladiola

(22) Which is the laziest mountain?

(23) How do mountains hear?

(24) What did the north wind say to the south wind?

ZANY RIDDLES

Answers: 22. Mt. Everest 23. With their mountain-ears 24. That's a breeze.

(25) What promise did the tsunami make to the tiny island?

(26) What did one tsunami say to another?

(27) What is the most impatient storm?

Answers: 25. Sea you soon! 26. That's swell! 27. A hurry-cane

FREAKS OF NATURE

28) What did the continental plate say after the earthquake?

29) What did the boy volcano say to the girl volcano?

30) Why did Zeus puff the clouds away?

ZANY RIDDLES

Answers: 28. It's not my fault. 29. Do you lava me like I lava you? 30. He wanted a blew sky.

FREAKS OF NATURE

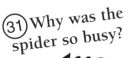

31 Why was the spider so busy?

32 What do you call a tiny bug that makes cloth?

33 What did the woman say to the bug with sandals on?

62

FREAKS OF NATURE

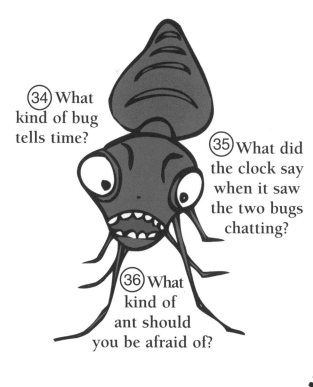

34 What kind of bug tells time?

35 What did the clock say when it saw the two bugs chatting?

36 What kind of ant should you be afraid of?

ZANY RIDDLES

(37) What did the drowned bug and the squashed bug have in common?

(38) Which insect is a natural ruler?

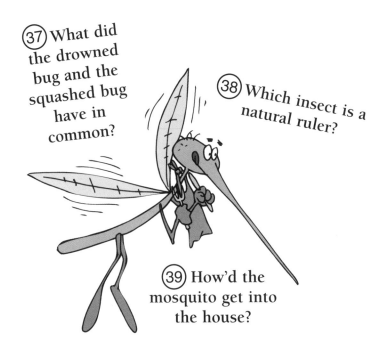

(39) How'd the mosquito get into the house?

Answers: 37. They were both under tow/toe. 38. The monarch butterfly 39. It passed its screen test.

GRaB BAg GooDies

ZANY RiDDLES

GRAB BAG GOODIES

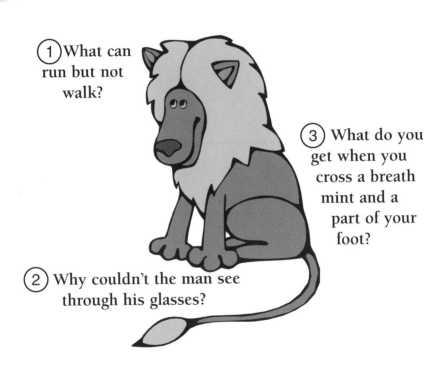

1) What can run but not walk?

3) What do you get when you cross a breath mint and a part of your foot?

2) Why couldn't the man see through his glasses?

Answers: 1. Water 2. There was still juice in them. 3. Tic Tac Toe

GRaB BAg GoOdieS

(4) What do you call the leader of yawners?

(5) What are the best spy shoes?

(6) Why couldn't the rapper fit into his limo?

ZANY RiDDLES

Answers: 4. *Chairman of the Bored* 5. *Sneakers*
6. *Because he was too phat.*

⑦ What kind of star is not in space?

⑧ What do you call a mediocre opera singer?

⑨ Why did the two magnets marry?

Answers: 7. A movie star 8. A so-so prano 9. Because the attraction was mutual.

GRAB BAG GOODIES

⑩ Why was the boy at the bottom of the well?

⑪ Why did the silly girl run through all her neighbors' yards?

⑫ What do you get when the silly knight eats a couple of toy boats?

ZANY RIDDLES

Answers: 10. Because he couldn't leave well enough alone. 11. She wanted to run the 50-yard dash. 12. Two ships that pass in the knight.

(13) What did one math book say to another?

(14) What kind of drum is not a musical instrument?

(15) What's both a musical instrument found in the house and a plate on the baseball field?

Answers: 13. You think you've got problems? 14. An ear drum 15. Home bass/base

GRAB BAG GOODIES

16 What musical instrument will help you catch fish?

17 How can you tell if a boat is friendly?

18 Why couldn't the foot feel anything when it stepped on the hot coal?

Answers: 16. Castanets 17. If it hugs the shore. 18. It was unnerved.

GRAB BAG GOODIES

19 What did the sock say when the seamstress mended it?

20 Why did the birthday boy fall over at his surprise party?

21 What do a groundhog and a lumberjack named Charles have in common?

Answers: 19. I'm the darndest thing. 20. He was floored. 21. They're both woodchucks.

GRAB BAG GOODIES

(22) Why was the exhausted kid sleeping next to the chopped-down tree?

(23) What day is the brightest day of the week?

(24) What day is perfect for pairs?

ZANY RIDDLES

Answers: 22. He was sleeping like a log.
23. Sun-day   24. Twos-day

GRAB BAG GOODIES

25) What's the best day to get married?

26) What's the best month for soldiers?

27) What's the best month for polite people?

Answers: 25. Wednesday, 26. March 27. May

28 What can you break without touching it?

29 What has two hands but no arms?

30 Which people were the greatest wanderers?

ZANY RIDDLES

GRAB BAG GOODIES

(31) Which people are always hurrying?

(32) What is both a piece of wood and a king?

(33) Which weighs more: a pound of wood or a pound of sand?

Answers: 31. The Russians
32. A ruler 33. They both weigh the same.

34 What did the silly grandmother give to the kid who asked for a heavy sweater?

35 Why is Cinderella lousy at basketball?

36 How can you tell that Robin Hood's arrows were scared?

ZANY RiDDLeS

Answers: 34. A sumo wrestler 35. She is always running away from the ball. 36. They were in a quiver.

(37) Why do dragons sleep all day?

(38) Why is everyone tired on April 1st?

(39) Which is faster: hot or cold?

Answers: 37. So they can fight nights. 38. Because it was a long March. 39. Hot—because you can catch cold!

GRAB BAG GOODIES

40 How did the snowman show he was mad?

41 When is a horseshoe bad luck?

42 What did one candle ask the other candle?

ZANY RIDDLES

Answers: 40. He turned a cold shoulder. 41. When you're the shoeless horse. 42. Are you going out tonight?

GRAB BAG GOODIES

43 Why did the invisible man go crazy?

44 What did one pair of glasses say to the other pair of glasses?

45 Why did Humpty Dumpty have a great fall?

Answers: 43. Out of sight, out of mind. 44. Stop making a spectacle of yourself. 45. To make up for a lousy summer.

(47) What's the difference between a crazy rabbit and counterfeit dollars?

(46) What holds up the moon?

(48) Why did the pirate put the chicken on the ground above his treasure?

ZANY RIDDLES

GRAB BAG GOODIES

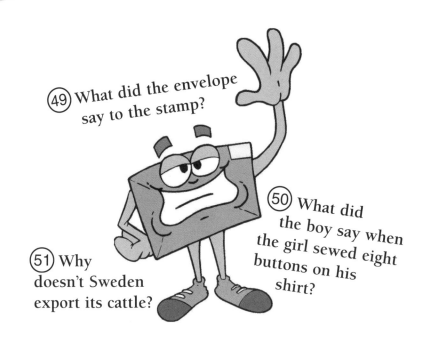

49 What did the envelope say to the stamp?

50 What did the boy say when the girl sewed eight buttons on his shirt?

51 Why doesn't Sweden export its cattle?

Answers: 49. Stick with me and we'll go places. 50. You fasten-eight-me. 51. Because it wants to keep its stock-home.

GRAB BAG GOODIES

(52) What is in fashion but out of date?

(53) What did the soccer ball say to the shoe?

(54) Why are movie stars cool?

ZANY RIDDLES

Answers: 52. The letter F. 53. I get a kick out of you.
54. Because they have so many fans.

GRaB BAg GoOdieS

55 Why are cemeteries so full?

56 How can you make varnish disappear?

57 If a leprechaun sits on a pot of gold, who sits on silver?

Answers: 55. Because people are dying to get in. 56. Take out the letter R. 57. The Lone Ranger.

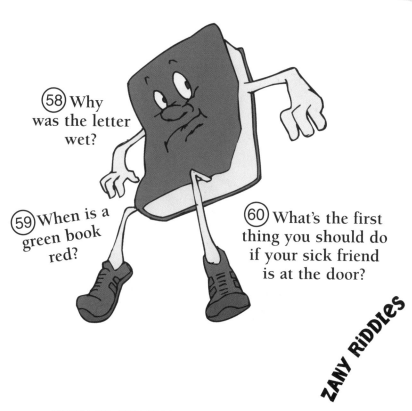

58) Why was the letter wet?

59) When is a green book red?

60) What's the first thing you should do if your sick friend is at the door?

ZANY RIDDLES

85

Answers: 58. It had postage dew. 59. When it's read. 60. Vitamin

GRAB BAG GOODIES

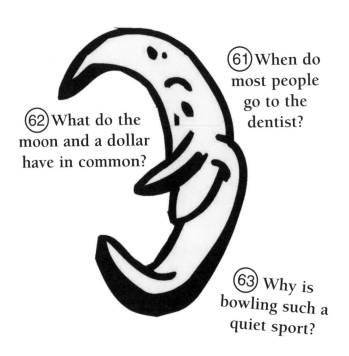

61) When do most people go to the dentist?

62) What do the moon and a dollar have in common?

63) Why is bowling such a quiet sport?

Answers: 61. Tooth-hurty. 62. They both have four quarters. 63. Because you can hear a pin drop.

(64) How can you make seven even?

(65) Why does underwear last forever?

(66) What has one horn and gives milk?

ZANY RiDDLES

Answers: 64. Take away the S.
65. Because it's never worn out. 66. A milk truck

(67) What has eyes but can't see?

(68) What's the hardest thing about learning to roller skate?

(69) Where do you sit at the ballpark if you want to keep your clothes white?

Answers: 67. Storms, potatoes and needles 68. The ground 69. The bleachers

⑦ What do a driver and a frog have in common?

⑦ What tiles shouldn't you stick to your walls?

⑦ Why are bells obedient?

ZANY RIDDLES

Answers: 70. Neither of them wants to be towed/toad. 71. Reptiles 72. They sound off when tolled.

GRAB BAG GOODIES

73. Why did it take so long for King Kong to swallow Big Ben?

74. What did one keyboard say to the other keyboard?

75. If April showers bring May flowers, what do May flowers bring?

Answers: 73. Because it was time-consuming.
74. You're not my type. 75. Pilgrims

GRaB BAg GoOdieS

76 What should you do if you don't feel well?

77 What's the Easter Bunny's favorite state capital?

78 What did the father light bulb say to its child?

ZANY RiDDLeS

Answers: 76. *Take off your mittens.* 77. *Albunny, NY*
78. *I wove you watts.*

(79) When do you want to catch flies but not hit them?

(80) What table has no legs?

(81) Why would the Easter Bunny be good at basketball?

Answers: 79. During a baseball game. 80. The multiplication table 81. He's good at stuffing baskets.

GRAB BAG GOODIES

82 The butcher was six feet tall, thin and busy. What did he weigh?

83 How does your bed get longer every night?

84 How did the pair of pants feel after being ironed?

ZANY RIDDLES

Answers: 82. Meat 83. You add feet to it. 84. Depressed

GRAB BAG GOODIES

85 Why don't people go to the moon for a holiday?

87 Why did the cowboy want a dachshund?

86 Why shouldn't you tell rumors about germs?

Answers: 85 It has no atmosphere. 86. You don't want to spread them around. 87. He wanted to get a long little doggie.

GRAB BAG GOODIES

88 What's the best month for gorillas?

89 On which day do you cook with oil?

90 Why was the mother glowworm unhappy?

ZANY RIDDLES

Answers: 88. Ape-ril 89. Fry day 90. Her children weren't that bright.

ABOUT THE AUTHOR

Erin Anthony lives with her family in Southern Illinois. She wants you to know that no animals were harmed in the writing of this book. She tested these riddles only on her son, whose groans in the laboratory seemed like a very good sign.